The Worth Within: 10 Practices to Transform Your Life and Reclaim Your Confidence

By Joycelyn Johnson, LPCC-s, LMHC

Introduction

What if I told you that your worth is not something you earn or achieve—it's something you already have, simply by being you? In a world that often equates value with success, productivity, or others' approval, it's easy to lose sight of this truth. Yet the journey to reclaiming your confidence and transforming your life begins with one powerful realization: *you are enough.*

Welcome to *The Worth Within,* a guide to uncovering, embracing, and living out your intrinsic value. This book isn't about quick fixes or perfection. It's about building sustainable habits that reinforce your self-worth and empower you to live authentically. The 10 practices in this book are tools to help you shift your mindset, practice self-compassion, and actively prioritize what truly matters—*you.*

Why This Book Matters
Many of us struggle with self-doubt, guilt, and the feeling that we're not measuring up. These feelings don't arise out of nowhere—they're shaped by life experiences, societal pressures, and even our own inner critic. But the good news is this: just as these feelings were learned, they can be unlearned.

The practices in this book are designed to help you take small, meaningful steps toward valuing yourself more. Whether it's reflecting on your achievements, setting healthy boundaries, or forgiving yourself for past mistakes, each chapter offers actionable steps to transform how you see yourself and how you show up in the world.

What to Expect
This book is divided into 10 chapters, each focusing on a key practice to help you reclaim your confidence and self-worth:

- **Reflect on Your Strengths and Achievements:** Discover the power of celebrating your progress, no matter how small.
- **Set Healthy Boundaries:** Learn to say no to what drains you and yes to what nurtures you.
- **Practice Self-Compassion:** Replace self-criticism with kindness and understanding.
- **Surround Yourself with Supportive People:** Build a circle of encouragement and limit toxic influences.
- **Take Care of Your Body and Mind:** Nurture yourself through healthy routines and mindfulness practices.

- **Pursue What Brings You Joy:** Reconnect with hobbies and passions that fulfill you.
- **Set Goals and Celebrate Progress:** Break goals into achievable steps and honor your milestones.
- **Forgive Yourself for Past Mistakes:** Let go of guilt and embrace your humanity.
- **Recognize Your Intrinsic Worth:** Affirm that your value is not tied to achievements or approval.
- **Seek Support if Needed:** Know when to reach out for help and the power of professional guidance.

Each chapter includes practical exercises, affirmations, and reflection prompts to help you integrate these practices into your daily life.

A Journey Worth Taking

Valuing yourself is not a destination—it's a lifelong journey. It's about learning to see yourself with compassion, recognizing your worth independent of external validation, and making choices that align with your inner truth. Along the way, you'll encounter challenges, but you'll also uncover a strength and resilience you didn't know you had.

This journey won't happen overnight, but every step forward matters. As you read this book, I encourage you to be patient with yourself. Celebrate the small wins, learn from the setbacks, and trust in your ability to grow.

You are enough. You have always been enough. And the practices in this book are here to help you remember and reclaim the worth that has been within you all along.

Let's begin.

Chapter 1: Reflecting on Your Strengths and Achievements

Have you ever paused to truly reflect on all the things you've done well? In the rush of life, it's easy to focus on what hasn't been accomplished yet, overlooking the moments of success and growth along the way. Learning to value yourself starts with acknowledging your strengths and achievements—both big and small—and celebrating how far you've come.

The Power of Reflection
Reflection is not about living in the past; it's about taking stock of your journey and recognizing the steps that have shaped who you are. Too often, we let doubt, fear, or the voices of others drown out our inner cheerleader. But reflecting on your strengths and achievements is a powerful way to quiet negativity and remind yourself of your unique value.

Think about the last time you felt proud of yourself. It could be landing a job, helping a friend in need, or simply getting through a tough day. Each of these moments matters because they reveal your resilience, creativity, and capacity to thrive. By focusing on your strengths, you begin to see yourself not through the lens of your struggles but as someone who consistently overcomes.

Making Your List
Start by taking some time to write down your strengths, talents, and achievements. Keep this process simple and genuine—there's no need for grand accomplishments to make the list meaningful. Sometimes, the most overlooked victories are the ones that deserve the most recognition.

Here's how to begin:
1. **Skills and Talents:** What are you naturally good at? Maybe you're a great problem-solver, an empathetic listener, or skilled at organizing chaos into order.
2. **Past Successes:** Reflect on moments when you felt accomplished. Did you finish a challenging project, support a loved one during a tough time, or learn something new? Write it down.

3. **Personal Growth:** Acknowledge areas where you've grown. Have you become more patient, learned to set boundaries, or found ways to manage stress better?

This exercise isn't just about what you've done—it's about who you are and the effort you've put into becoming that person.

Celebrating the Small Wins

Sometimes we get caught up in waiting for big, defining moments to validate our worth. But the truth is, small wins are just as important. Did you manage to take care of yourself during a particularly tough week? Did you call a friend when you felt like isolating? These are victories.

Small wins create momentum, and celebrating them builds confidence. When you acknowledge your progress, no matter how modest it seems, you train your mind to look for the positive instead of dwelling on perceived shortcomings.

Recognizing Progress Over Perfection

Another key to valuing yourself is shifting your focus from perfection to progress. It's easy to dwell on what's left to accomplish or where you think you've fallen short. But by reflecting on how far you've come, you shift the narrative to one of growth rather than deficiency.

Ask yourself:
- Where was I a year ago? How have I changed or improved since then?
- What challenges have I faced, and what strengths did I use to overcome them?
- What habits or mindsets have I developed to support my growth?

This shift in focus is empowering because it moves you away from a scarcity mindset ("I haven't done enough") and toward abundance ("Look at what I've achieved!"). It's a reminder that progress is a journey, not a destination.

A Practice of Gratitude for Yourself

Finally, as you reflect, practice gratitude for the person you are. You are the sum of your strengths, achievements, and even your mistakes. Gratitude reinforces self-worth because it's a way of saying to yourself, "I see you, and I appreciate all that you've done and all that you are."

Try this exercise:
- At the end of each day, write down one thing you did well. It could be as simple as completing a task you'd been putting off or choosing kindness when it would have been easier not to.
- Revisit your list regularly to remind yourself of your progress.

Conclusion
Reflecting on your strengths and achievements is a form of self-love. It's a chance to honor your unique journey and recognize that you are not defined by what you lack but by the richness of what you've already achieved. So take a moment today to make your list, celebrate your wins, and shift your focus toward how far you've come. Your journey matters, and so do you.

Chapter 2: Setting Healthy Boundaries

Boundaries are the invisible lines that protect your time, energy, and well-being. They aren't about shutting others out but rather about defining what's acceptable in your life and prioritizing your needs without guilt. Setting healthy boundaries is one of the most empowering steps toward valuing yourself, yet it's also one of the hardest, especially if you're used to putting others first.

Learning to Say No

Many of us struggle with saying no. Whether it's out of fear of disappointing others, a desire to be liked, or the simple habit of overcommitting, saying yes to everything can leave you drained and resentful. But every time you say yes to something that doesn't align with your values or capacity, you're effectively saying no to yourself.

Learning to say no is not selfish; it's self-respect. It's acknowledging that your energy is finite and that you deserve to use it in ways that serve you. Here's how to begin practicing this essential skill:

1. **Recognize Your Limits:** Be honest about how much time, energy, and emotional bandwidth you have. Overextending yourself benefits no one.
2. **Be Clear and Direct:** When declining a request, you don't have to over-explain. A simple, "I can't commit to this right now" is enough.
3. **Prepare for Pushback:** Some people may resist your boundaries, especially if they're used to you always saying yes. That's okay. Their reaction is about them, not you.

By saying no to things that drain you, you're making room for the things that truly matter—your priorities, your passions, and your peace.

Prioritizing Yourself

When was the last time you put yourself first without guilt? Society often praises selflessness, especially in caregivers and nurturers, but prioritizing yourself is not only healthy—it's necessary. You cannot pour from an empty cup.

Here's how to begin making yourself a priority:
1. **Identify What Nurtures You:** What activities bring you joy, relaxation, or a sense of fulfillment? Whether it's reading, walking in nature, or spending quiet time alone, make these non-negotiable parts of your routine.
2. **Schedule Self-Care:** Treat self-care as an appointment you can't cancel. Block out time for rest, exercise, hobbies, or even doing nothing.
3. **Let Go of Guilt:** Understand that prioritizing yourself isn't selfish; it's an act of self-preservation. When you care for yourself, you show up better for others.

Recognizing Boundary Violations

Sometimes, people may test or ignore your boundaries. This could look like:
- A friend repeatedly asking for favors even after you've said no.
- A coworker expecting you to take on tasks outside your job description.
- A family member who doesn't respect your need for space.

When this happens, it's important to reinforce your boundaries calmly but firmly. Use statements like:
- "I understand you need help, but I'm not available for that right now."
- "I've already explained that I can't take this on. Please respect my decision."
- "I need some time to myself, and I hope you can understand."

Holding your boundaries may feel uncomfortable at first, especially if you're not used to advocating for yourself. But over time, it becomes easier, and you'll notice a growing sense of confidence and peace.

The Benefits of Healthy Boundaries
When you set and uphold boundaries, you're doing more than just managing your relationships—you're reclaiming your power. Here are some of the rewards of establishing healthy boundaries:
- **More energy and time:** By saying no to what doesn't serve you, you free up resources for what truly matters.
- **Improved relationships:** Boundaries foster mutual respect and prevent resentment from building up.
- **Greater self-worth:** Each time you enforce a boundary, you reinforce the belief that you are deserving of respect and care.
- **Reduced stress:** With clear boundaries, you no longer feel stretched thin or taken advantage of.

Practical Boundary-Setting Tips
1. **Start Small:** Practice setting boundaries in low-stakes situations to build confidence.
2. **Communicate Early:** The sooner you establish boundaries, the easier they are to maintain.
3. **Use "I" Statements:** Frame your boundaries in terms of your needs. For example, "I need time to recharge after work, so I won't be able to talk until later."
4. **Enforce Consequences:** If someone repeatedly violates your boundaries, consider limiting your interaction with them.

Conclusion
Setting healthy boundaries is a declaration of your worth. It's a way of saying, "I value my time, energy, and well-being, and I deserve relationships and commitments that honor those things." By learning to say no and prioritizing yourself, you take an important step toward living authentically and thriving in every aspect of your life.
Remember: boundaries aren't barriers—they're bridges to a healthier, happier you.

Chapter 3: Practicing Self-Compassion

Self-compassion is one of the greatest gifts you can give yourself. It's the practice of extending kindness and understanding to yourself in moments of struggle, failure, or pain. Yet for many, being compassionate to oneself feels unnatural. Negative self-talk, perfectionism, and the fear of being seen as "weak" often stand in the way. But self-compassion isn't about being weak or letting yourself off the hook—it's about acknowledging your humanity and treating yourself with the same care and understanding you would offer a dear friend.

Challenging Negative Self-Talk

The way you speak to yourself matters. Negative self-talk—those harsh, critical voices in your mind—can wear you down and make you feel unworthy. You might catch yourself thinking things like, "I'll never get this right," or "I'm not good enough." These thoughts not only damage your confidence but also prevent you from seeing your strengths.

Practicing self-compassion starts with recognizing and challenging these patterns. Instead of allowing self-criticism to go unchecked, try reframing those thoughts with affirmations and more balanced perspectives. Here's how:

1. **Notice the Negative Talk:** Pay attention to moments when you are overly critical of yourself. Awareness is the first step to change.
2. **Pause and Reflect:** Ask yourself, "Would I say this to a friend who's going through the same thing?" If not, it's a sign to adjust your tone.
3. **Replace Criticism with Affirmations:** When you catch a negative thought, counter it with a kinder, more realistic affirmation. For example:
    - Instead of, "I can't do anything right," try, "I'm doing the best I can with what I have."
    - Instead of, "I'm such a failure," try, "I've hit a rough patch, but I'll find a way through this."

With practice, these affirmations can become a natural part of your inner dialogue, replacing negativity with encouragement.

Treating Yourself Kindly

Imagine your closest friend comes to you feeling defeated after making a mistake. How would you respond? Likely, you'd reassure them, remind them of their strengths, and offer your support. Why, then, is it so hard to extend the same grace to yourself?

Treating yourself kindly involves adopting the same compassionate attitude you would have toward someone you love. It's about understanding that you, like everyone else, are imperfect and worthy of kindness regardless of the circumstances.

Here are ways to cultivate this practice:
1. **Use Gentle Language:** When things don't go as planned, avoid harsh words like "stupid" or "lazy." Instead, say things like, "This didn't work out, but I'm learning and growing."
2. **Acknowledge Your Efforts:** Even if the outcome isn't perfect, give yourself credit for trying. Effort is a reflection of your courage and determination.
3. **Give Yourself Permission to Feel:** It's okay to feel frustrated, sad, or overwhelmed. Rather than judging yourself for these emotions, remind yourself that they're part of being human.

The Three Pillars of Self-Compassion

According to self-compassion expert Dr. Kristin Neff, self-compassion has three key components:
1. **Self-Kindness vs. Self-Judgment:** Be kind and understanding toward yourself rather than harshly critical.
2. **Common Humanity vs. Isolation:** Recognize that everyone experiences struggles and that you're not alone in your challenges.
3. **Mindfulness vs. Over-Identification:** Be mindful of your feelings without becoming consumed by them.

These pillars provide a foundation for approaching life's difficulties with more gentleness and resilience.

The Benefits of Self-Compassion

Self-compassion isn't just about feeling better—it has tangible benefits for your overall well-being. When you practice self-compassion:

- **Your stress decreases:** Being kind to yourself helps calm your inner critic and reduces anxiety.
- **Your resilience grows:** You're more likely to bounce back from setbacks because you approach them with understanding rather than self-blame.
- **Your relationships improve:** When you treat yourself kindly, you're more likely to extend the same kindness to others.

Practical Exercises to Build Self-Compassion

1. **Write a Self-Compassion Letter:** Imagine you're writing to a friend who's facing the same struggles as you. Offer them encouragement, support, and understanding. Then read the letter back to yourself.
2. **Practice Daily Affirmations:** Start your day by repeating affirmations like, "I am enough," or "I am worthy of love and respect."
3. **Use the Mirror Technique:** Look in the mirror and say something kind to yourself, such as, "You've been through so much, and I'm proud of you for showing up."

Conclusion

Practicing self-compassion is a powerful way to shift your relationship with yourself. By challenging negative self-talk and treating yourself with kindness, you create an inner environment where you can thrive. Remember, self-compassion isn't about perfection—it's about embracing your humanity, flaws and all. Be gentle with yourself, and watch as your sense of self-worth grows stronger every day.

Chapter 4: Surrounding Yourself with Supportive People

No one thrives in isolation. The people around us shape our thoughts, attitudes, and beliefs—often more than we realize. Surrounding yourself with supportive people is an essential part of valuing yourself and living a fulfilling life. These are the individuals who lift you up, inspire you to grow, and remind you of your worth even when you forget it yourself. Equally important is learning to distance yourself from toxic influences that drain your energy and undermine your confidence.

The Power of Encouragement

Supportive people are like the sunshine in your garden of growth— they nurture your spirit and fuel your potential. These are the friends, family members, mentors, or colleagues who see your strengths even when you can't. They listen without judgment, offer encouragement, and celebrate your successes as if they were their own.

To seek out more encouragement in your life:
1. **Identify Uplifting People:** Reflect on the people in your life who make you feel good about yourself. Who inspires you to be your best self? Spend more time with them.
2. **Be Open to New Connections:** Sometimes, the most supportive relationships come from unexpected places. Join groups or communities that align with your interests or values to meet like-minded individuals.
3. **Ask for What You Need:** Don't be afraid to ask for support or encouragement. A simple, "I'm going through a tough time— can we talk?" can open the door to meaningful conversations and connection.

Being surrounded by encouraging people doesn't mean relying on them to make you feel good about yourself; it means fostering relationships that remind you of your strengths and potential when you need a boost.

The Cost of Toxic Influences

Just as supportive people help you grow, toxic influences can stifle your progress. These are the individuals who constantly criticize, belittle, or manipulate you, leaving you feeling drained or unworthy. While it's not always easy to walk away from toxic relationships, creating distance is an act of self-preservation.

Here's how to manage toxic influences:
1. **Recognize the Signs:** Pay attention to how you feel after interacting with someone. Do you feel anxious, unworthy, or drained? These could be signs of a toxic relationship.
2. **Set Clear Boundaries:** Establish limits on what you will and won't tolerate. For example, you might say, "I can't continue this conversation if it becomes disrespectful."
3. **Limit Interaction:** Reduce the time you spend with people who bring negativity into your life. This might mean cutting back on calls, texts, or visits—or ending the relationship altogether if necessary.
4. **Replace with Positivity:** As you create distance from toxic influences, fill the space with uplifting relationships or activities that bring you joy.

Remember, distancing yourself from toxic people isn't about blaming or resenting them; it's about protecting your well-being and creating a space where you can thrive.

Building a Circle of Support

Creating a supportive network doesn't happen overnight, but small, intentional steps can make a big difference. Here's how to build a circle of support:
1. **Be Selective:** Choose people who align with your values and genuinely care about your well-being.
2. **Invest in Relationships:** Support is a two-way street. Show up for others in the same way you want them to show up for you.
3. **Stay Connected:** Make time for regular check-ins with the people who matter most. Whether it's a phone call, coffee date, or quick text, these moments strengthen your bond.

Your circle of support doesn't need to be large. A few genuine, encouraging relationships can have a greater impact than dozens of superficial ones.

The Benefits of a Supportive Network

When you surround yourself with supportive people, the effects ripple through every area of your life. You may notice:
- **Increased confidence:** Encouragement from others helps you see yourself through a more positive lens.
- **Emotional resilience:** A strong support system makes it easier to weather challenges and setbacks.
- **Greater motivation:** Being around inspiring people pushes you to pursue your goals and dreams.
- **Improved well-being:** Supportive relationships reduce stress and promote a sense of belonging.

Balancing Support and Self-Reliance

While having supportive people in your life is invaluable, it's also important to cultivate self-reliance. Support from others should enhance your sense of worth, not replace it. Strive for a balance where you feel secure both in your relationships and within yourself.

Conclusion

The company you keep profoundly influences your self-worth and overall happiness. By seeking encouragement from supportive people and limiting toxic influences, you create an environment where you can grow and thrive. Surround yourself with those who believe in you, inspire you, and remind you of your inherent value. Remember: the people in your life should make you feel loved, respected, and empowered to be the best version of yourself. Choose them wisely.

Chapter 5: Taking Care of Your Body and Mind

Taking care of your body and mind is an act of self-love and a cornerstone of personal well-being. When you prioritize your physical health and mental balance, you lay the foundation for a more confident, joyful, and productive life. This chapter explores how establishing healthy routines and embracing mindfulness can nurture both your body and your inner self.

Building Healthy Routines

Your body is your home, and taking care of it is essential to living a full and vibrant life. Healthy routines—such as sleeping well, eating nourishing food, and staying active—can transform the way you feel physically and mentally.

1. Prioritize Quality Sleep Sleep is more than just rest; it's the time when your body repairs itself and your mind processes the events of the day. Lack of sleep can lead to irritability, reduced focus, and even long-term health issues.

- **Create a Sleep Schedule:** Aim to go to bed and wake up at the same time each day, even on weekends.
- **Design a Relaxing Nighttime Routine:** Wind down with calming activities like reading, taking a warm bath, or listening to soothing music.
- **Limit Screen Time:** Turn off electronics at least an hour before bed to reduce exposure to blue light, which can interfere with your body's natural sleep rhythms.

2. Nourish Your Body with Food What you eat has a direct impact on your mood, energy levels, and overall health. A balanced diet fuels your body and mind, helping you feel your best.

- **Choose Whole Foods:** Opt for fruits, vegetables, lean proteins, whole grains, and healthy fats.
- **Stay Hydrated:** Drink plenty of water throughout the day to keep your body functioning optimally.
- **Practice Mindful Eating:** Pay attention to your meals by savoring each bite, eating slowly, and avoiding distractions like TV or smartphones.

3. Incorporate Movement Exercise isn't just about physical fitness; it's a powerful tool for boosting mood, relieving stress, and building self-esteem.

- **Find What You Enjoy:** Whether it's dancing, walking, swimming, or yoga, choose activities that make you happy and keep you moving.
- **Set Realistic Goals:** Start small and build gradually. Even a 10-minute walk can make a difference.
- **Make it Fun:** Exercise with friends, listen to music or podcasts, or try new activities to keep things interesting.

Practicing Mindfulness

While taking care of your body is important, nurturing your mind is equally vital. Mindfulness practices such as meditation and journaling help you connect with your inner self, reduce anxiety, and create mental clarity.

1. Embrace Meditation - Meditation isn't about emptying your mind—it's about becoming aware of your thoughts and feelings without judgment. Even a few minutes a day can make a big difference.

- **Start Small:** Begin with just 5 minutes a day in a quiet space.
- **Focus on Your Breath:** Pay attention to your inhale and exhale, letting it anchor you in the present moment.
- **Try Guided Meditations:** Use apps or online videos to guide you through the process.

2. Explore Journaling - Journaling is a powerful way to process your emotions, reflect on your experiences, and clarify your thoughts.

- **Start with Gratitude:** Write down three things you're grateful for each day to cultivate a positive mindset.
- **Express Freely:** Use your journal to vent frustrations, celebrate wins, or explore dreams without worrying about grammar or structure.
- **Set Intentions:** Write about your goals and the steps you can take to achieve them.

3. Practice Being Present - Mindfulness isn't limited to meditation or journaling—it's a way of life. Practice being present during everyday activities, whether it's savoring your morning coffee, listening fully to a friend, or noticing the sights and sounds around you.

Benefits of Taking Care of Your Body and Mind

When you commit to caring for yourself holistically, you'll begin to notice the benefits in every area of your life:

- **Improved Mood:** A healthier body and a calmer mind reduce stress and increase happiness.
- **Boosted Self-Esteem:** When you prioritize your well-being, you send a message to yourself that you are worthy of care and respect.
- **Greater Resilience:** Healthy routines and mindfulness build the physical and emotional strength needed to face life's challenges.

Practical Tips for a Balanced Life

- **Set Realistic Expectations:** Don't aim for perfection—focus on consistency. Small steps add up over time.
- **Create a Routine That Works for You:** Customize your healthy habits and mindfulness practices to fit your lifestyle and preferences.
- **Celebrate Your Progress:** Acknowledge your efforts and progress, no matter how small. Every step toward self-care is a victory.

Conclusion

Taking care of your body and mind is not a luxury; it's a necessity. Healthy routines provide the energy and strength to live your best life, while mindfulness nurtures a deeper connection to yourself and the present moment. By making your well-being a priority, you honor your worth and pave the way for a life filled with vitality, balance, and joy. You are your greatest investment—take care of yourself accordingly.

Chapter 6: Pursue What Brings You Joy

Joy is the essence of a meaningful life, yet it's often neglected in the hustle and bustle of daily responsibilities. Pursuing what brings you joy is not just a luxury—it's a necessity for your emotional and mental well-being. Engaging in hobbies and exploring your passions allows you to reconnect with your true self, bringing fulfillment, creativity, and happiness into your life.

Engage in Hobbies That Fulfill You
Hobbies are more than just pastimes; they are opportunities to unwind, recharge, and express yourself. When you engage in activities you love, you create a sense of balance and purpose that can enhance all aspects of your life.

1. Identify What Sparks Joy: Think about the activities that make you lose track of time. Is it painting, gardening, reading, cooking, or playing an instrument? Maybe it's something you enjoyed as a child but haven't revisited in years. Whatever it is, let it guide you toward what fulfills you.

2. Make Time for Your Hobbies: Life's demands can make it feel impossible to carve out time for yourself, but prioritizing your hobbies is an act of self-care. Schedule dedicated time in your week for the things you love. Even 30 minutes a day can make a significant difference.

3. Share Your Hobbies with Others: Sharing your interests with like-minded people can deepen your enjoyment and create a sense of community. Join clubs, attend workshops, or simply invite friends to join you in your favorite activities.

4. Try Something New: If you're unsure what hobbies might fulfill you, don't be afraid to experiment. Take a pottery class, try yoga, or learn a new language. The key is to explore without judgment or pressure to be perfect.

Explore Your Passions

Passions go beyond hobbies—they are the pursuits that give your life deeper meaning and purpose. When you allow yourself to follow your interests, you open the door to self-discovery and personal growth.

1. Listen to Your Inner Voice: What excites you? What have you always wanted to try but never made time for? Pay attention to the moments that light you up and follow those instincts. Your passions often align with your values and strengths.

2. Use Your Talents: Your unique talents and skills can be powerful tools for pursuing your passions. Whether it's writing, mentoring, teaching, or creating, use your gifts to enrich your life and the lives of others.

3. Step Outside Your Comfort Zone: Pursuing your passions often involves taking risks. Whether it's signing up for a course, starting a side project, or volunteering for a cause you believe in, embrace the challenges as opportunities to grow.

4. Give Back: Sometimes, your passion can be found in helping others. Volunteering, mentoring, or contributing to your community can bring a profound sense of fulfillment and purpose.

The Benefits of Pursuing Joy

Engaging in hobbies and exploring your passions brings numerous benefits to your overall well-being:

- **Enhanced Mental Health:** Doing what you love reduces stress, boosts happiness, and helps you stay present.
- **Increased Confidence:** Mastering a new skill or pursuing a passion reinforces your self-belief and sense of accomplishment.
- **Stronger Connections:** Hobbies and passions often connect you with like-minded individuals, fostering deeper relationships.
- **Renewed Energy:** Joyful activities provide a break from routine, leaving you refreshed and motivated.

Overcoming Barriers to Joy

It's easy to put off pursuing joy because of time constraints, guilt, or self-doubt. Here are ways to overcome these barriers:

- **Let Go of Guilt:** Remember, taking time for yourself isn't selfish—it's necessary for your well-being.
- **Start Small:** You don't need hours of free time to pursue joy. Begin with small, manageable steps, like reading one chapter of a book or practicing a skill for 15 minutes.
- **Make it Non-Negotiable:** Treat your hobbies and passions as important as any other responsibility. Schedule them into your calendar and honor that time.

Living a Joyful Life

Pursuing what brings you joy isn't about abandoning your responsibilities; it's about weaving fulfillment into your everyday life. Joy is what sustains you through challenges and helps you appreciate the beauty of the present moment. When you allow yourself to engage in hobbies and explore passions, you create a life that feels meaningful and aligned with who you truly are.

Conclusion

Life is too short to ignore the things that make your heart sing. Pursue what brings you joy with intention and enthusiasm. Whether it's through hobbies, passions, or discovering new interests, make room for what lights you up. When you prioritize joy, you enrich not only your own life but also the lives of those around you. Follow your heart, embrace your passions, and watch as your world becomes brighter and more fulfilling.

Chapter 7: Set Goals and Celebrate Progress

Setting goals gives your life direction, and celebrating progress fuels your journey forward. When you approach your ambitions with intentionality and joy, you create a sense of purpose and momentum. Breaking goals into manageable steps and recognizing every milestone along the way transforms the process from overwhelming to empowering.

Why Goals Matter

Goals are like a map for your life—they guide your actions, shape your decisions, and provide clarity about where you're headed. Whether you're striving for personal growth, career advancement, or improved well-being, setting meaningful goals helps you stay focused and motivated.

However, the journey to achieving goals isn't always straightforward. That's why breaking them into smaller steps and celebrating progress is essential. These practices keep you grounded, optimistic, and resilient, even when challenges arise.

Breaking Goals into Steps

Big goals can feel daunting, but breaking them into smaller, manageable steps makes them achievable. This approach also gives you a sense of accomplishment along the way, keeping you motivated.

1. Define Your Goal: Be clear and specific about what you want to achieve. A well-defined goal is easier to pursue. For example:

- Instead of "I want to be healthier," try "I want to walk for 30 minutes five days a week."

2. Break It Down: Divide your goal into smaller, actionable steps. For example, if your goal is to write a book, your steps might include:

- Brainstorming ideas
- Outlining chapters
- Writing 500 words per day
- Revising one chapter at a time

3. Set Timelines: Assign deadlines to your steps to keep yourself accountable. Realistic timelines provide structure without adding unnecessary pressure.

4. Start Small: Focus on one step at a time. Each small win builds confidence and momentum, making the larger goal feel more attainable.

The Importance of Celebrating Progress

Progress is often overlooked in the pursuit of big achievements. But every milestone, no matter how small, is a step forward and deserves recognition. Celebrating progress reinforces positive habits, boosts motivation, and makes the journey more enjoyable.

1. Acknowledge Your Effort: It's not just about the outcome—it's also about the effort you put in. Whether you complete a step or simply stay consistent, take a moment to appreciate your hard work.

2. Celebrate Milestones: Identify key milestones along the way and reward yourself when you reach them. For example:
- After completing the first draft of a project, treat yourself to your favorite meal.
- When you meet a fitness goal, buy new workout gear or take a relaxing day off.

3. Share Your Success: Sharing your progress with supportive friends or family members can make the celebration even sweeter. They'll cheer you on and remind you of how far you've come.

4. Reflect on Growth: Progress isn't always linear, but each step teaches you something valuable. Take time to reflect on how you've grown, what you've learned, and how you've overcome challenges.

Overcoming Challenges

Even with the best plans, obstacles are inevitable. Here's how to stay on track:
- **Stay Flexible:** If a step doesn't go as planned, adjust your approach. Flexibility is key to progress.
- **Reframe Setbacks:** View challenges as opportunities to learn rather than failures. Each hurdle you overcome strengthens your resilience.

- **Keep Your Eye on the Prize:** Remind yourself why you set the goal in the first place. Reconnecting with your "why" can reignite your motivation.

Benefits of Setting Goals and Celebrating Progress
When you take the time to set clear goals and recognize your achievements, you experience:
- **Increased Focus:** Clear goals help you prioritize what matters most and eliminate distractions.
- **Boosted Confidence:** Celebrating milestones reinforces your belief in your ability to succeed.
- **Sustained Motivation:** Progress, no matter how small, fuels your desire to keep going.
- **Greater Enjoyment:** Recognizing growth makes the journey rewarding, not just the destination.

Practical Tips for Success
- **Write It Down:** Putting your goals on paper makes them tangible and keeps you accountable.
- **Track Your Progress:** Use a journal, app, or checklist to monitor your steps and milestones.
- **Reward Yourself Meaningfully:** Choose rewards that genuinely make you happy, whether it's a relaxing day off, a small gift, or time spent with loved ones.
- **Celebrate Consistency:** Sometimes, simply sticking to your plan is worth celebrating, even if the progress feels slow.

Conclusion
Setting goals and celebrating progress is a journey of growth and self-discovery. By breaking goals into manageable steps, you make them achievable, and by celebrating your milestones, you stay motivated and energized. Remember, every step forward is progress, and every moment of celebration strengthens your resolve. Your dreams are worth pursuing, and the path to achieving them is just as important as the destination. Keep going—you're closer than you think!

Chapter 8: Forgive Yourself for Past Mistakes

Forgiving yourself for past mistakes is one of the most freeing acts you can do for your well-being. Mistakes are an inevitable part of being human, yet many of us carry guilt and self-blame long after the moment has passed. Learning to let go and embrace your imperfections allows you to focus on the present and move toward a brighter future.

Mistakes Are Part of Being Human

No one goes through life without making mistakes. Whether big or small, mistakes are a natural part of learning, growing, and navigating an imperfect world. Yet, we often hold ourselves to unrealistic standards, expecting perfection where it doesn't exist.

1. Accept Your Humanity: Being human means being fallible. Mistakes are not a reflection of your worth but evidence that you are trying, learning, and living. Remind yourself that everyone—no matter how successful—has stumbled along their journey.

2. Reframe Mistakes as Lessons: Instead of viewing mistakes as failures, see them as opportunities to grow. Ask yourself:

- What can I learn from this experience?
- How can I use this lesson to make better choices moving forward?

This mindset shift transforms mistakes into valuable stepping stones rather than barriers.

The Weight of Guilt

Guilt can feel like a heavy chain, anchoring you to the past. While it's natural to feel regret after a mistake, holding onto guilt for too long serves no purpose. It keeps you stuck in a cycle of self-criticism and prevents you from embracing the present.

1. Acknowledge Your Emotions: Before you can let go of guilt, it's important to acknowledge it. Allow yourself to feel the weight of your emotions without judgment. Writing about your feelings in a journal or talking to a trusted friend can help you process them.

2. Recognize What's Beyond Your Control: Some mistakes arise from circumstances outside your control. Take responsibility for your role, but don't blame yourself for things you couldn't foresee or prevent.

3. Replace Guilt with Self-Compassion: Speak to yourself as you would to a friend who is feeling guilty. Would you say, "You're a terrible person," or would you offer words of kindness and understanding? Practice extending that same compassion to yourself.

Letting Go and Moving Forward
Letting go of guilt doesn't mean forgetting what happened—it means releasing its hold on you so you can move forward. Forgiving yourself allows you to live fully in the present and create a better future.

1. Apologize and Make Amends: If your mistake impacted others, take steps to apologize and make amends where possible. Owning up to your actions can bring closure and demonstrate your commitment to growth.

2. Focus on the Present: Guilt keeps you tethered to the past, but the present moment is where change happens. Practice mindfulness to center yourself in the here and now, letting go of regrets that no longer serve you.

3. Create a Vision for the Future: What do you want your life to look like moving forward? Set intentions or goals that reflect the lessons you've learned and the person you aspire to become.

The Power of Self-Forgiveness

Forgiving yourself is not an act of weakness—it's an act of strength. It means acknowledging your imperfections without letting them define you. When you release guilt and embrace self-forgiveness, you free yourself to live with greater peace and purpose.

Practical Steps to Forgive Yourself
1. **Write a Forgiveness Letter:** Write a letter to yourself acknowledging the mistake, expressing regret, and offering forgiveness. You don't have to share it with anyone—it's a private act of healing.
2. **Repeat Forgiveness Affirmations:** Affirmations like "I am worthy of forgiveness" or "I release the guilt I've been carrying" can help rewire your mindset.
3. **Celebrate Your Growth:** Reflect on how you've changed since the mistake. Celebrate the resilience and courage it took to face your challenges and grow from them.

Benefits of Forgiving Yourself

Self-forgiveness has profound benefits for your mental, emotional, and even physical health:
- **Reduced Anxiety:** Letting go of guilt alleviates the mental burden that often accompanies it.
- **Improved Relationships:** When you forgive yourself, you're more likely to extend forgiveness and understanding to others.
- **Increased Confidence:** Releasing self-blame allows you to step into your power with renewed self-assurance.
- **Greater Inner Peace:** Self-forgiveness creates space for healing and allows you to focus on what truly matters.

Conclusion

Forgiving yourself for past mistakes is one of the greatest gifts you can give yourself. Mistakes are not the end of the story—they're just chapters in the larger narrative of growth and resilience. By letting go of guilt and embracing your humanity, you open the door to a future full of possibility. You are more than your past—your present and future are waiting for you to claim them.

Chapter 9: Recognize Your Intrinsic Worth

In a world that often equates worth with achievements, productivity, or others' opinions, it's easy to lose sight of the truth: your worth is intrinsic. It's not something you earn or prove—it's something you simply *are*. Recognizing your intrinsic worth means embracing yourself fully, flaws and all, and understanding that you are enough just as you are.

Affirming Your Worth Daily

Affirmations are powerful tools for reshaping your mindset and silencing the critical inner voice that tells you you're not enough. By repeating positive statements, you remind yourself of your inherent value and begin to internalize self-acceptance.

1. Start Your Day with Affirmations: Begin each morning with affirmations that reinforce your worth. Look in the mirror and say:
- "I am enough."
- "I deserve love and respect."
- "My value is not tied to what I do, but to who I am."

Starting your day this way sets a positive tone and helps you carry self-assurance into everything you do.

2. Personalize Your Affirmations: Tailor affirmations to what resonates most with you. If you struggle with self-doubt, affirm, "I trust myself and my decisions." If you seek confidence, try, "I am capable and worthy of success."

3. Repeat Often: Affirmations aren't one-and-done; they require consistency.
Write them down, post them where you'll see them daily, or even record yourself saying them to listen back.

Valuing Yourself Beyond Achievements
Modern society often sends the message that your worth is tied to what you accomplish. Promotions, accolades, and the approval of others may feel validating, but they are not the foundation of your self-worth. True value comes from within.

1. Separate Your Worth from Productivity Your accomplishments are a reflection of your skills and efforts, not your value as a person. Whether you succeed or fail, your worth remains constant. Recognize that rest, relaxation, and simply *being* are just as valid as working hard or achieving goals.

2. Define Yourself by Your Qualities, Not Your Outcomes: Instead of focusing on what you've done, consider who you are. Are you kind? Resilient? Creative? Compassionate? These qualities define your essence and contribute to your worth in ways that no external measure can.

3. Stop Seeking External Validation: While praise from others can feel good, relying on it to affirm your worth is a slippery slope. Practice self-validation by acknowledging your own efforts and celebrating your strengths, regardless of external feedback.

Practicing Self-Worth
Recognizing your intrinsic worth requires intentional practice, especially if you've spent years trying your value to external factors. Here are practical ways to embrace your worth:

1. Reflect on Your Inner Strengths - Write down qualities you admire in yourself. Are you patient, empathetic, or determined? Keep this list visible to remind yourself of your inherent value.

2. Treat Yourself with Respect - Respect yourself through your actions. Speak kindly to yourself, set boundaries to protect your time and energy, and make decisions that align with your values.

3. Celebrate Your Existence - Your worth is not dependent on doing or achieving—it's in your very being. Celebrate small joys, your presence, and the relationships you cherish. Simply existing is enough to make you valuable.

The Impact of Recognizing Your Intrinsic Worth

When you embrace your intrinsic worth, you experience profound shifts in how you view yourself and interact with the world:

- **Increased Confidence:** Knowing you are enough reduces self-doubt and empowers you to pursue your goals without fear of failure.
- **Stronger Boundaries:** Valuing yourself helps you set boundaries that protect your well-being and preserve your energy.
- **Healthier Relationships:** When you recognize your worth, you attract and maintain relationships built on mutual respect and care.
- **Inner Peace:** Letting go of the need for external validation brings a sense of calm and contentment.

Overcoming Challenges

It's natural to have moments of doubt, especially if you've internalized beliefs that tie your worth to external factors. When those moments arise:

- **Challenge Negative Thoughts:** Replace "I'm not good enough" with "I am worthy as I am."
- **Seek Support:** Surround yourself with people who uplift and affirm your worth.
- **Practice Patience:** Recognizing your worth is a lifelong journey, and it's okay to take small steps.

Conclusion

Recognizing your intrinsic worth is a powerful act of self-love and liberation. It allows you to live authentically, free from the pressures of perfection and the need for constant validation. By affirming your value daily and embracing the truth that your worth is not tied to your achievements or others' approval, you create a life rooted in confidence, peace, and self-acceptance. Remember: you are enough—always.

Chapter 10: Seek Support if Needed

Sometimes, no matter how much effort you put into building self-esteem and valuing yourself, the struggles persist. This isn't a sign of weakness—it's a sign of being human. Seeking support during these moments is an act of courage and self-care. Professional help, such as therapy or counseling, can provide the tools and insights you need to uncover deeper issues and create lasting change.

Why Professional Support Matters
Self-esteem struggles often stem from complex and deeply rooted experiences, such as past trauma, unresolved emotions, or long-standing negative beliefs about oneself. While self-help strategies can be effective, a therapist or counselor brings expertise and objectivity that can guide you in ways you might not achieve on your own.

1. Uncover Deeper Issues: A trained professional can help you explore the origins of your self-esteem struggles. They can identify patterns, triggers, or past events that contribute to how you view yourself today. Understanding these underlying issues is the first step toward healing and growth.

2. Develop Personalized Strategies: Therapists use evidence-based techniques to help you rebuild self-worth and develop healthier thought patterns. These strategies are tailored to your unique experiences and needs, making them more effective than one-size-fits-all solutions.

3. Provide a Safe Space: Therapy offers a judgment-free environment where you can openly express your feelings, fears, and struggles. This safe space allows you to confront challenges you might otherwise avoid and process them constructively.

Signs You May Benefit from Support
Not everyone who struggles with self-esteem needs therapy, but there are certain signs that seeking professional help could be beneficial:
- **Persistent Negative Self-Talk:** You can't shake feelings of inadequacy, even when things are going well.
- **Difficulty Letting Go of the Past:** Past mistakes or traumatic experiences continue to affect your self-worth.

- **Struggles With Relationships:** Low self-esteem impacts how you interact with others, leading to unhealthy dynamics or isolation.
- **Feeling Stuck:** Despite your efforts, you feel unable to make progress or sustain improvements in how you value yourself.

If you resonate with these signs, reaching out for support could be a transformative step forward.

What to Expect from Therapy

For those new to therapy, the process can feel intimidating, but understanding what to expect can ease those concerns.

1. Initial Assessment: Your therapist will begin by getting to know you, your history, and your goals for therapy. This helps them understand your unique situation and create a plan tailored to your needs.

2. Collaborative Goal-Setting: You'll work with your therapist to define clear, realistic goals. For example, you might want to build confidence, challenge negative beliefs, or learn to set boundaries.

3. Tools and Techniques: Depending on your needs, your therapist may use techniques such as:
- **Cognitive Behavioral Therapy (CBT):** To identify and reframe negative thought patterns.
- **Mindfulness Practices:** To help you stay present and reduce anxiety.
- **Self-Compassion Exercises:** To cultivate kindness toward yourself.

4. Progress Over Time: Therapy is a journey, not a quick fix. Celebrate small wins along the way as you begin to notice shifts in how you think, feel, and interact with the world.

Finding the Right Therapist

The relationship between you and your therapist is crucial to the success of therapy. Take the time to find someone who aligns with your needs and makes you feel comfortable.

1. Research Options: Look for licensed therapists who specialize in self-esteem, self-worth, or related issues. Many therapists list their areas of expertise on their websites or directories like Psychology Today.

2. Ask Questions: During an initial consultation, ask questions to determine if they're a good fit:
- What is your approach to helping clients with self-esteem struggles?
- What can I expect from our sessions?
- Do you have experience working with people with similar concerns?

3. Trust Your Instincts: Choose someone you feel safe with. A good therapist will create an environment where you feel heard, supported, and respected.

Overcoming Barriers to Seeking Help

It's normal to feel hesitant about seeking therapy. You might worry about stigma, costs, or whether your struggles are "serious enough." Here's how to overcome those barriers:
- **Reframe Therapy as Self-Care:** Just as you'd see a doctor for physical health, therapy is an investment in your mental and emotional well-being.
- **Explore Affordable Options:** Many therapists offer sliding scale fees, and community mental health centers or online platforms provide cost-effective alternatives.
- **Validate Your Feelings:** Your struggles are valid, no matter how "small" they may seem. Therapy isn't just for crises—it's for growth.

The Impact of Seeking Support

Seeking professional help can be life-changing. With the guidance of a therapist or counselor, you'll:

- **Gain Clarity:** Understand the root causes of your self-esteem struggles and how to address them.
- **Build Resilience:** Develop tools to navigate challenges and setbacks with confidence.
- **Foster Self-Worth:** Learn to value yourself authentically, independent of external validation.

Conclusion

Seeking support when self-esteem struggles persist is not a sign of failure but a declaration of your commitment to yourself. Therapy can provide the tools, insights, and encouragement you need to uncover your intrinsic worth and live a life of confidence and self-respect. Remember, asking for help is one of the strongest and most loving things you can do for yourself—you deserve it.

NOTES

List of resources to help you shift your mindset, practice self-compassion, and build habits that affirm your self-worth:

Books
1. **"The Gifts of Imperfection" by Brené Brown**
   - Focuses on embracing your imperfections, practicing self-compassion, and living wholeheartedly.
2. **"Self-Compassion: The Proven Power of Being Kind to Yourself" by Dr. Kristin Neff**
   - A foundational guide on self-compassion, backed by research and practical exercises.
3. **"Atomic Habits" by James Clear**
   - Helps you build habits that reinforce your worth and align with your goals.
4. **"Daring Greatly" by Brené Brown**
   - Explores how vulnerability and self-acceptance can lead to greater confidence and connection.
5. **"Radical Acceptance: Embracing Your Life with the Heart of a Buddha" by Tara Brach**
   - Guides readers in accepting themselves fully and letting go of judgment.

Online Courses
1. **The Science of Well-Being (Yale University via Coursera)**
   - A free course designed to help you increase happiness and build healthy habits.
2. **Self-Compassion: The Proven Power of Being Kind to Yourself (Kristin Neff on Sounds True)**
   - Online courses and meditations focused on cultivating self-compassion.
3. **Mindfulness-Based Stress Reduction (MBSR) Programs**
   - Available online, these programs teach mindfulness practices that foster self-acceptance.

Podcasts
1. **"The Happiness Lab" with Dr. Laurie Santos**
   - Focuses on science-backed strategies to build happiness and self-worth.
2. **"Therapy Chat" with Laura Reagan**
   - Discusses topics like self-compassion, self-worth, and emotional healing.

3. **"Unlocking Us" by Brené Brown**
   - o Explores vulnerability, courage, and the importance of valuing yourself.

Apps
1. **Calm**
   - o Offers guided meditations and mindfulness practices to foster inner peace and self-compassion.
2. **Insight Timer**
   - o Free meditation app with a focus on self-worth, gratitude, and affirmations.
3. **ThinkUp**
   - o Allows you to create and listen to personalized affirmations daily.

Support Groups and Communities
1. **Meetup Groups**
   - o Look for local or virtual groups focused on personal growth, self-compassion, or mindfulness.
2. **The Self-Compassion Community by Dr. Kristin Neff**
   - o A supportive community for people practicing self-compassion.
3. **Facebook Groups**
   - o Search for groups on self-improvement, self-love, and mindfulness.

Workbooks
1. **"The Mindfulness and Self-Compassion Workbook" by Kristin Neff and Christopher Germer**
   - o Provides exercises to integrate mindfulness and self-compassion into daily life.
2. **"The Self-Love Workbook" by Shainna Ali**
   - o A practical guide to building self-esteem and practicing self-love.
3. **"The Self-Esteem Workbook" by Glenn R. Schiraldi**
   - o Focuses on building resilience and a positive self-image.

Therapeutic Resources

1. **BetterHelp or Talkspace**
   - Online therapy platforms where you can work on self-esteem and mindset with a licensed therapist.
2. **Psychology Today Therapist Finder**
   - Search for local therapists specializing in self-esteem, self-compassion, and mindset shifts.

Websites and Blogs

1. **Self-Compassion.org (Dr. Kristin Neff)**
   - Resources, exercises, and guided meditations to foster self-compassion.
2. **Mindful.org**
   - Articles and resources on mindfulness practices that support emotional well-being.
3. **Tiny Buddha**
   - Offers articles, stories, and tips for self-love, self-worth, and personal growth.

YouTube Channels

1. **Therapy in a Nutshell (Emma McAdam)**
   - Practical tips for improving mental health and building self-worth.
2. **The Holistic Psychologist (Dr. Nicole LePera)**
   - Videos on healing, self-awareness, and self-empowerment.
3. **Brené Brown's Talks**
   - Her TED Talks and interviews focus on vulnerability, courage, and embracing imperfections.

Affirmation and Journal Tools

1. **"Five-Minute Journal"**
   - A daily journal for practicing gratitude and affirming your worth.
2. **Daily Affirmation Decks**
   - Card decks like "Affirmators!" provide fun, uplifting affirmations to boost your confidence.

These resources offer practical tools, inspiration, and guidance to help you shift your mindset, embrace self-compassion, and actively affirm your worth. Start small, and choose the ones that resonate most with your needs and goals.

www.ingramcontent.com/pod-product-compliance
Lightning Source LLC
Chambersburg PA
CBHW051923250726

48659CB00002B/800